EXTREME MACHINES
ON LAND

PATRICIA ARMENTROUT

The Rourke Press, Inc.
Vero Beach, Florida 32964

Patricia Armentrout specializes in nonfiction writing and has had several book series published for primary schools. She resides in Cincinnati with her husband and two children.

PHOTO CREDITS:
© Scott Cambell/Intl. Stock: Cover, page 10; © Corel Corporation: pages 4, 6, 16; © Warren Faidley/Intl Stock: page 19; © Mark E. Gibson/Intl. Stock pg. 18; © Vincent Graziani/Intl. Stock: page 21; © NASA: page 15; © Marilyn Newton: page 12; © Jeff Osborne: pages 9, 22; © Dusty Willison/Intl. Stock: page 7; © SSC Programme LTD/Jeremy Davey: page 13

EDITORIAL SERVICES:
Penworthy Learning Systems

Library of Congress Cataloging-in-Publication Data

Armentrout, Patricia, 1960-
    Extreme machines on land / Patricia Armentrout.
       p. cm. — (Extreme machines)
    Includes index.
    Summary: Briefly describes some unusual land vehicles, such as all-terrain vehicles, Indy cars, jet cars, dragsters, tanks, and solar cars.
    ISBN 1-57103-211-8
    1. Motor vehicles—Juvenile literature. [1. Motor vehicles.]
I. Armentrout, Patricia. 1960- II. Title III. Series: Extreme machines.
TL147.A75 1998
629.2—dc21   98–20294
                                                      CIP
                                                      AC

Printed in the USA

TABLE OF CONTENTS

LAND MACHINES

What do monster trucks, rocket cars, dirt bikes, and **locomotives** (LO kuh MO tivz) have in common? They are all extreme land machines.

An extreme machine can be huge, like a locomotive, or small, like a dirt bike. An extreme machine is extreme because it can do something most other machines cannot do. Extreme machines go beyond normal limits.

An extreme machine in action.

OFF-ROAD VEHICLES

Imagine driving a machine up steep hillsides, through mud pits, or across a sandy desert. Some machines are made to do just that.

Dirt bikes, **all-terrain** (AWL tuh RAYN) vehicles, and some trucks are built to handle the extreme conditions found on off-road trails.

All-terrain vehicles are tough enough to handle the ups and downs.

Dirt bike riders spend as much time in the air as they do on the ground.

A powerful motor, a rugged **suspension** (suh SPEN shun), and big tires help these vehicles perform at their best in the worst conditions. Some drivers test themselves and their machines in off-road races held all over the world.

LOCOMOTIVE

A locomotive is an engine that pulls or pushes a train. Trains can have one car or as many as 200 cars.

Most locomotives are run by powerful diesel engines. Some use electricity that comes from a cable or rail high above the track. One electric train in France broke a speed record when it reached 320 miles (515.2 kilometers) an hour.

The newest locomotive is called a **maglev** (MAG lev). Electric magnets allow the train to float above the rail. Because the maglev floats, it is very smooth and very fast.

This huge locomotive can pull millions of pounds of freight.

INDY CAR

One of the most popular car races in the United States is the Indianapolis 500. The race is held during the Memorial day weekend each year. The cars that race in the Indianapolis 500 are called Indy cars.

Indy cars are not your average family car. They sit low to the ground and have powerful engines. The engine is behind the driver's seat. A special fuel called **nitromethane** (NY tro METH ayn) is used for maximum engine power.

As you may have guessed, the race is 500 miles (805 kilometers) long. Thousands of fans watch as the Indy cars go over 200 miles (322 kilometers) an hour around the track.

Indy cars sit low and hug the track as they race to the finish line.

JET CAR

A jet car is an extremely fast machine. A jet engine, like the kind on military fighter jets, powers the car. Race car drivers compete for the land speed record in jet cars.

The Thrust jet car speeds across the desert at over 700 miles an hour.

A jet car is built for speed.

A jet car is launched, like a missile, across land. Jet cars reach speeds greater than 700 miles (1,127 kilometers) an hour!

Parachutes are used to slow down a jet car before the wheel brakes bring the car safely to a complete stop.

CRAWLER-TRANSPORTER

The crawler-transporter is a unique machine. It was built for National Aeronautics Space Administration (NASA) and is used to carry space shuttles from their hanger to the launch pad.

The crawler-transporter has two crawlers that have eight tracks. Each crawler weighs about three thousand tons (2,700 metric tons). The crawler-transporter stands 20 feet (6.1 meters) high and is the size of a baseball diamond.

The crawler-transporter creeps about one mile (1.6 kilometers) an hour with a space shuttle aboard, and close to two miles (3.2 kilometers) an hour unloaded.

NASA's crawler-transporter may move slowly; but it is a big, powerful machine.

DRAGSTER

A drag race is one of the shortest races you will ever watch. The fastest dragsters are called top fuel cars. They can go over 300 miles (483 kilometers) an hour and finish the race in less than 5 seconds.

Drag racing is an expensive sport. A top fuel dragster costs about $160,000. Taking care of the car costs even more. A drag racing team can easily spend a million dollars to compete for one season. Corporate sponsors pay most of the expenses in this extreme sport.

A drag race is over in the blink of an eye.

MILITARY TANK

A tank is a mean, tough-looking machine. Tanks travel through almost any terrain. They use tractor treads, which are tracks wrapped around sets of small wheels. Tracks make it almost impossible for a tank to get stuck in mud.

A tank's heavy armor helps to protect its crew from enemy attack.

An M-1 main battle tank is ready for combat training.

Tanks are protected by heavy armor. The armor helps keep the crew safe from enemy attack. Most tanks have a powerful gun mounted on a moveable **turret** (TER it). Special computers help the tank crew pick their target and fire a round of **ammunition** (AM yuh NISH un).

19

SOLAR CAR

A solar car runs on energy from the sun. Solar-powered cars look nothing like gasoline-powered cars. One design named Aurora II weighs a little over 500 pounds (226.5 kilograms) and has only three wheels.

Solar cars are equipped with **solar cells** (SO lur SELZ). Solar cells convert the sun's energy into electricity. Batteries store the electricity that powers the car.

Solar energy is safe for the **environment** (en VY run ment). More solar cars could be seen in the future if improvements are made to solar cell and battery designs.

Solar cars operate best on bright sunny days.

GLOSSARY

all-terrain (AWL tuh RAYN) — a vehicle suitable for any surface

ammunition (AM yuh NISH un) — explosive things fired from guns

environment (en VY run ment) — surroundings

locomotives (LO kuh MO tivz) — railroad engines that pull or push railroad cars

maglev (MAG lev) — a magnetic levitation train; a high-speed train that moves along a track by electric magnetic force

nitromethane (NY tro METH ayn) — an engine fuel used in top fuel dragster race cars

solar cells (SO lur SELZ) — devices that collect and convert the sun's energy into electricity

suspension (suh SPEN shun) — equipment such as springs and shock absorbers found on motorized vehicles

turret (TER it) — a revolving structure on which guns are mounted

It takes a powerful machine to pull heavy train cars through the mountains.

INDEX

FURTHER READING

Find out more about Extreme Machines with these helpful books:
Dregni, Michael. *The Indianapolis 500.* Capstone Press Minneapolis, 1994.
Sosa, Maria. *Dragsters.* Crestwood House, 1987.
Wood, Sydney. *Trains and Railroads.* Dorling Kindersley, Inc., 1992.